The Job Seeker Manifesto

The Job Search Marketing Plan:

Declare to the World How You Will Find
Your Next Job!

By

Katherine Burik and Dan Toussant

Job Talk Press,

4911 LeighAvenue NW,

Canton, OH 44709

Print ISBN: 978-0-9893787-2-7
Adobe PDF: 978-0-9893787-1-0
ePUB: 978-0-9893787-0-3

Cover Design and Illustration by: Little Pond Creative
Book Design by Martha Fewell
Development Editing by Siddique Qureshi
Final Editing by Martha Fewell
Book Production by Bookmasters Inc

The Job Seeker Manifesto

The Job Search Marketing Plan:
Declare to the World How You Will Find Your Next Job!

DEDICATION – Katherine Burik

Writing a book is a new experience for me. I like it! I like organizing my thoughts around a subject I love in a way I hope you will understand.

Many people supported this effort. My husband Kermit put up with my energy and focus on something other than him. My kids Marissa, Dan, and Brett let me practice on them. My sister Martha was willing to try something new. My coach, mentor, and friend Sherry Greenleaf pushes me at the right time. My partner Dan Toussant is the best business partner I could ever ask for.

Carolyn James was the original Interview Doctor and a great friend and mentor. As a recruiter, many great and awful candidates passed through her doors. She tried to help each one. Some needed more help than others so she passed them along to me for the professional coaching that allowed candidates to shine. Thank you Carolyn!

DEDICATION – Dan Toussant

To Nan and Jeff, thanks for the introduction. The Interview Doctor partnership Katherine and I offer people wanting to make a job change or career change has been a real gift to both of us, and only possible because of you.

For all the candidates we have coached through the Interview Doctor, thanks for sharing your career planning and job-seeking challenges. Coaching is a teaching business, and when you teach, you learn at a deeper level; what we share in this book and the others to follow, we know – when it comes to job seeking: this is what works best.

And, to all of my family, especially Colleen, thanks for your strong support and your reliable love.

Contents

About This Series and How to Read This Book

Finding a new job can be hard. It can also be a rewarding and enlightening experience. Depends on how you approach the search.

After talking to many candidates at The Interview Doctor and in our previous lives as human resource executives and recruiters in corporate America, we know candidates have some of the same problems.

We have some tricks that can help.

The trick to a successful job search is to have a plan to distinguish yourself from other candidates. You have to be able to explain who you are or what you have to offer. No one can figure that out for you. But most candidates have absolutely no idea where to begin.

The series The Job Seeker Manifesto offers a step-by-step strategic approach to finding a job including many tricks we learned through extensive experience throughout our careers. All the stories we share are true, reflecting real job seekers we worked with through The Interview Doctor.

If you see yourself in these pages, it is because many people have similar problems finding a job. We changed the names to protect our clients' privacy.

This is the first book in a five book series digging deep into five areas of job search, starting with 1) creating a strategic plan, then 2) creating the tools necessary to display your talents including resumes and your LinkedIn profile, 3) strategically designing how you describe yourself starting with the critical question, "tell me about yourself", 4) interviewing smartly, and finally 5) closing the deal.

Pick the topic or two that address your particular issue or read the entire series, depending on your specific needs and interests.

This first book lays the groundwork for your job search. Every big adventure begins with a plan. So start your job search by creating a plan that reflects what you want and what you will do every day, week and month.

Write in the margins. Take notes. Create worksheets. Challenge yourself to understand what you want then go after your dream.

Use these books to give yourself a head start over other candidates and find the job you love.

The Job Seeker Manifesto

A manifesto is a declaration, a statement, a philosophy about what you intend. Every job search starts with a declaration of what you want and why you should have what you want. You must understand what makes you uniquely suited for the job you want. Your manifesto provides a unique approach to your job search reflected in your job search marketing plan, the tools you choose, and the way you choose to describe yourself to others.

First, you need a Job Search Marketing Plan to outline the core elements of your job search. By putting energy and thought into a plan in the beginning, you can focus on how to get what you want during your search.

A solid Job Search Marketing Plan has five steps:

- **Explore:** Define the jobs that fit you and your career goals and interests.
- **Define:** Know who you are and what you bring to the table. Figure out what you want in your next job, the type of work, the type of environment, preferred industries, where that job will be located, and size of the company.

- **Network:** Seek out and connect with people who can help you get what you want.
- **Refine and Articulate:** Know what you want people to know about yourself.
- **Conclude:** Get what you want

This book covers the concepts of "Explore," "Define," and "Network." Future books will explore concepts in "Refine and Articulate"; including the tools you need during your job search and how to win at interviews.

The techniques we offer can apply to young and old, professional and laborer, executive and office worker. The trick is making a plan that works for you, understanding who you are and what you have to offer, then working the plan until you get what you want. The principles are simple. But it is hard work. Your results are based on the effort you put in. We know it works.

Let's get started.

Chapter 1

Job Seekers Take Many Forms.

Bill's Story
Bill loves his profession but hates his boss.

> *I got into finance and accounting early on. In high school, I excelled in math so I majored in business in college. I was the treasurer of my fraternity for a while. I started investing early and by college, I had a pretty good track record so I decided to go into finance because I loved the way I could look at a pile of information and figure out what it meant and how to use it to make great outcomes. Finance really fits me well.*

> *But this company really stinks. My boss is an absolute jerk. I can't make heads or tails of him. He is unpredictable. One day he is nice, the next day he is mean. He humiliates people when he yells at them in front of the group. You have to do exactly what he*

wants you to do even if there is a better way. He can never be wrong. He makes me miserable. I go home at night dreading to come to work the next day. On Sunday night, I get stomachaches and can't sleep at all because I am filled with dread. The worst part is my boss likes me.

I can't seem to get away from this guy. I can't see a better path in this company although I like the company and I am getting recognized for my contribution. I just have to get away from this jerk.

I have not looked for a job in at least ten years. The economy is bad right now and I am sure no one is hiring. I do not know how to change jobs but I am committed to getting out of here.

What should I do?

Bill is about 32 years old and must have good skills to be recognized and promoted in his company. He has not begun networking and in fact never goes to any business related meetings outside of his company. He doesn't think he knows anyone. Bill put together a resume and responded to a few ads but nothing has happened.

The diagnosis? Bill needs a plan. He would benefit from some expert help from The Interview Doctor. He has not connected the dots to create a job search strategy as part of any kind of plan. He does not yet value networking and he thinks responding to ads is an effective technique for finding his next job. He needs help.

Jessica's Story
Jessica is still employed as a sales person but wants to sell something else. She believes this is possible but does not know exactly what she wants or how to offer her sales experience in a different industry.

> *I love my job. Selling is my thing. I love getting close to people. I love meeting different personalities and understanding how to help that person. That is the sales challenge to me. I think the time is right to get out of selling real estate and move into selling something else. My job is not in jeopardy so that is a good thing. I am getting frustrated trying to find which industry is best for me. I don't know how to contact the right people. I am sending out resumes but not making any progress."*

> *Jessica is a 39-year-old college graduate with a background in health care management*

and chemistry. In her current role, she sells retirement living to seniors. She makes good commission but wants to sell something else, maybe pharmaceutical or medical supplies sales. She is having trouble making the transition.

Jessica talked to a recruiter who recommended that she call The Interview Doctor to figure out what she is doing wrong. I got the call. I asked Janice what she wants. She stumbled and stammered through a response. It is clear she does not know exactly what she wants. She does not have a LinkedIn account and is not comfortable networking.

The diagnosis? Jessica knows she wants to work in sales. That is a start. But, she has not narrowed down the field sufficiently to know which industries and companies she should target. She does not have the basic networking structure in place to support her job search. She will not get far and will continue to be frustrated unless she addresses this problem. She needs a *Job Search Marketing Plan.*

Tom's Story

Tom was just laid off from a really great job as a Supply Chain Manager for a large manufacturing company.

Impossible. I can't believe this is happening to me. Not today. Not after what I have contributed to this company. I can't believe it. How will I tell Susan? How will we pay the bills? I am not sure what to do next."

Tom is 52 years old with a wife, Susan, and three children, one still in college, one in high school and one grown daughter who just graduated from college. Tom had six jobs with strong career advancement with several different companies. His latest company, XYZ Plastics recently merged with another plastics company. The new Vice President selected someone else for this role so he was terminated. Tom received some severance but not enough to carry him for long. Susan's job does not pay enough to support the family. He needs to find a job quickly but he doesn't know where to start.

Tom has a resume but he is not sure how good it is and he is not exactly sure if he wants to continue with this career. He has gotten feedback from a few people about his resume but the feedback is conflicting and he is not sure what to do. He submitted his resume for a few openings he found on Monster and got one callback but nothing happened. He doesn't really know where to look.

He is starting to get depressed and lose confidence.

A friend suggests he contact The Interview Doctor for help.

I got the call. "Let's catch a cup of coffee and talk about what you want and what we can do for you." Tom sent me his resume prior to their meeting. The resume looks ok but nothing special. Not much about the resume makes Tom stands out from other people who work in supply chain and logistics.

The diagnosis? Tom doesn't have a plan. He doesn't know what he wants. As with anything else, without a plan you will never get where you want to go. Every job seeker, whether currently employed or out of work, needs a **Job Search Marketing Plan.**

Bill, Jessica, and Tom are not unique. Perhaps you have been in their shoes before.

Reasons to change jobs.
People change jobs all the time for many different reasons. Sometimes you can choose when you change jobs and sometimes someone or something else helps you decide. It is always better to be in charge of your own destiny, but that is not always possible.

The way you come to the idea of changing jobs is not as important as what you do after you decide (or someone decides for you). You need courage and confidence. You need support from your friends and family. You need good advice. You need a plan.

What do you do after you've been laid off?

Being laid off has its own challenges because the experience leaves marks that must be addressed before you put together your plan.

I've been through layoffs more times than I care to say. Things at work are unusually quiet for a few weeks. Then you are called to a meeting in the boss's office. He looks grim. Maybe he is with someone for morale support. He says he has bad news.

Your position has been eliminated. It is not personal; it is just business. His lips are moving but all you hear is blah, blah, blah. He gives you an envelope and asks you to clean out your personal things or come in on the weekend to pick them up if you prefer to leave now.

You are not sure what to do. All you know is you have to get out of there – they want you to leave and you just want to sink into the floor.

1. Take everything from your office/work space that is even remotely yours. Once you leave, you will not generally have access again. Especially make sure you have any files from your computer that are yours, like your contact lists and personal files. Do not take anything that belongs to the company. Don't worry about pictures and such. You can pick these up later or they can be sent to your home.

2. Leave the premises. You can say good-bye later via email or phone.

3. Collect yourself. This is a very difficult emotional blow. Take a minute to allow yourself to cry. Maybe have a drink when you get somewhere you are safe.

4. Find your spouse, parent, or significant other. You need someone to lean on.

5. Read the paperwork you received. Determine how much severance the company is offering, if they are offering any at all. Find a knowledgeable friend to discuss what is appropriate.

6. Contact the designated company representative to negotiate a better settlement if it is possible. Don't forget to collect any unused vacation or sick time. Every little bit helps.

7. Do not start your job search yet. Let a few days pass to let the news sink in.

8. Figure out what you want to do next. Give this some thought.

9. Then start your Job Search Marketing Plan, targeting what you want to do and how you plan to go about getting what you want.

I am kind of an expert at this. I am not sure that should be a point of pride. I have been laid off a number of times. Each time for different reasons – company went under, position was redundant, and once when a new president preferred someone else to handle my function.

My husband and I have been married for 18 years and it seems one or the other of us has been laid off in many of those years. In fact, we have a joke that only one of us is allowed to be out of work at a time. After a while, you just get used to the idea that a job is no longer a permanent thing.

The bottom line is to remain calm, don't do anything you will regret later. Go home and cry for no more than three days. It is natural to be sad, especially about your lack of control or perhaps what you might have done differently to change the outcome. But, don't wallow in it. Put on your big-kid pants and get on with your career. You will find a workplace and people who value you more than those yo-yo's. I promise.

Just like the song, I pick myself up, brush myself off, and start all over again..[i] The trick is getting back your confidence by having a plan to keep you focused.

Changing Careers

Not everyone looking for a job has been laid off. Perhaps you want to be promoted, or you are looking for a better position while still employed, or you are leaving college or returning to the workforce after raising children. Whatever your reason, the advice is the same. Know what you want, have a plan, and move forward confidently!

Chapter 2

Job Search Marketing Plan

Every project has a plan. Every day has a plan, even if the plan is to have no plan.

Most Saturday mornings you wake up and probably think for a moment about what you want to do on the weekend. Maybe you need to go to the grocery store, get more dog food, wash the car, and visit your mom. Many people scribble notes on a scrap of paper with the stuff to pick up at the grocery store, maybe the order you want to do the chores. And voila, you have a plan!

The kind of plan you outline for yourself is a reflection of your personal style. It could be as simple as a scrap of paper or as complex as a multi-page project plan with a Gantt chart. But everyone has a plan.

Non-plans do not help

Every job seeker has a plan. It is just that some "plans" are vague, unformed, and unproductive. Let us call that a "non-plan". It is a plan, yes, but mostly ineffective; a non-plan is exactly the kind of plan that guarantees your job search takes forever.

In a non-plan job search, the candidate, let's call him Henry, checks the newspaper (maybe the real paper kind) and perhaps the ad consolidators on the Internet for jobs related to his/her job function. Henry sends out resumes in response to the ads. Then sits back and waits for the phone to ring. He gets more and more frustrated. Henry watches his unemployment checks wither away along with his savings. His embarrassment over his predicament makes him second-guess his every move. His confidence takes a nose-dive. If he is called for an interview, Henry barely keeps his chin off his shoes apologizing for his very existence, not listening, and not knowing how to display his skills and background in a way that makes him stand out against his competition. Henry and others like him can be out of work for a long, long time.

Plans are just lists of choices and decisions that must be made. The candidate with a "non-plan" made specific choices along the way. Unfortunately, they are choices and decisions that sidetracked the search. Let's consider:

- Choosing to answer ads instead of more effective search techniques
- Not really knowing what he wants or where to find it
- Not effectively using his time
- Not understanding what he offers employers or how to express it
- Allowing his situation to impact his self-confidence

A "non-plan" is a bad plan. Do yourself a favor and make a real plan that works for you instead of against you.

Plans have steps

According to A Guide to the Project Management Body of Knowledge (PMBOK Guide) from the Project Management Institute, a project plan is a process by which someone accomplishes a goal. You must understand the goal and decide which steps are necessary to achieve the goal.

Your plan may be simple or complex with many details. At a minimum, to get where you want to go you must know what you want and what you are willing to do to get it. It is also good to understand why that goal is the right goal for you.

A plan is like a map. If you don't have a map, you are traveling blind.[ii] You might get there eventually but there will be a lot of costly twists and turns in the road, costing money, time, or energy. With a map, you know where you are going, which roads get you there faster, and you can recognize the right place when you are there.

Businesses put together marketing plans to sell cereal, services, or machinery. They want to understand who is the competition, who is likely to buy this product, how much can it be sold for, where can it be sold, who are the people to talk to about buying the product, and other important information about the marketplace and the buyers. Then they measure themselves against the key milestones to see how well they accomplish the goal.

A Job Search Marketing Plan for a job seeker is a marketing plan in which the product to be sold is you. It is amazing how job seekers, even those in sales and marketing, overlook this simple idea. You are the product.[iii]

Scott's Story

Scott was an Interview Doctor client who specialized in sales. His job search was stalled and he did not understand why. He applied for job after job in his targeted field but nothing happened. He was starting to think it was his age or the way he dressed, a sign that his extended search was wearing on his confidence.

After talking with him for a short while about his goals and interests and about marketing in general he stopped talking for a second. He said, "Are you telling me that a job search is just like sales? Have I missed the point this whole time? If so then I already know how to do this."

It occurred to him that the techniques that he used every day to market and sell truck parts were exactly the same techniques he could use to sell himself to a new employer. He got off the phone with renewed excitement and confidence. A week later he called with the good news; he found a job! In that short time after our call he identified his potential marketplace and contacts, started calling his contacts, renewed a relationship with a former customer and was offered a job!

It doesn't always happen as neatly as it did with Scott but the point is the same. With a plan, you can understand your marketplace.

Stephen Covey, in his groundbreaking book <u>The</u> *7 Habits of Highly Effective People*[iv], says that highly effective people begin with the end in mind (Habit #2). Begin with a clear picture of where you are now and where you are going. In this way, your steps always take you in the correct direction – the direction that takes you to your goal.

You must understand what you want in order to put all your energy to finding *it* then convincing the people who own it that they should give it to you. So, your plan begins with a goal and has steps along the way to achieving the goal.

Individual plans may vary but essentially the steps include:

1. **Goal** – what do you want, what does it look like, where is it located (in general), why is this important to you, what will it feel like when you get it
2. **Research** – Which companies and people can you talk to about that job
3. **Understand** what you have to offer – why are you the right person for this kind of a job
4. **Prospect** – talk to as many people and companies as you can until you find people willing to talk with you about your goal
5. **Make your case** – clearly explain the fit, build relationships until they find you irresistible
6. **Close the deal**

Without a plan, you will wander all over. We frequently hear from candidates who have no plan.

Lila's Story

> Lila is a boating friend I see in the summer. In May, on the first weekend at the boat, I asked how she was doing. She explained she had been laid off from her job at a doctor's office. She submitted application after application over the winter but got no response. Her plan, if you can call it a plan, was to respond to ads until something good happened. I asked what she wanted. She was willing to take almost anything.

How long do you think it will take Lila to get a job? Using her current approach, it will take Lila a very long time. She did no planning, she does not know what she wants, she does not know who to talk to or where to find the right job, and she is not using methods that will produce the result she wants. It takes a long time to get somewhere if you don't know where you going or how to get there.

Chapter 3

Explore what you want to do next

Every plan begins with a goal. As with any big project, if you do not define the goal, you will never know if you achieve the outcome you want. Start by defining what you want.

Kayla's Story

> Kayla was, recently laid off from her employer after more than twenty years of progressively more responsible positions with the same employer. She is a strong, successful person but now she wonders if there is something else out there for her.

Is it okay to NOT follow the path she was on before? Two competitors have already approached her so she could jump right back in if she wanted. A small voice in the back of her mind is telling her not to do that, to take some time to find something different.

It is okay want to take time before jumping back into the work pool right away. Maybe the first thing to do after leaving your job is choosing to not update your resume. Updating your resume means you want to continue doing what you have been doing. Maybe what you have been doing is not right for you anymore. But, how do you know what you want to do next?

Daydream.

Where do your thoughts take you? What do you like to do with your spare time? Are there any thoughts or activities that come up more often? What activities make you smile and what activities would you scoop dog poop in the yard to avoid doing? (My personal measure!)

Kayla's Story

> *Kayla has always worked with building materials. Her husband is a contractor. They own rental property. So, while she was healing in the first few weeks after the layoff, she fixed up an apartment that had been empty for two years. It took her ten days and she finally got the apartment rented. She found an unexpected sense of accomplishment and pride. She also found it easy. So now she is thinking maybe she can develop a career that*

centers around real estate; maybe commer-cial real estate. She will let the experience percolate while she daydreams some more about her future. We will see what happens!

Kayla is taking a little time to explore what she wants so she can create a career that makes her happy, pays the bills, and builds on her skills and interests.

Understand what you are good at.
As a parent, I think my daughter, Marissa, is wonderful. She is smart, passionate, and gets to the heart of issue with good solutions. But truth be told, she is not always easy to work with. Employers and teachers have told her this before! I've told her this before! She finally seems happy in her latest job because she works alone on detailed work on which she is an expert and only needs to talk to people on her own terms. She is thrilled!

She finally found the right combination of tasks, people, and responsibilities that match her interests and style. Marissa found a position that exploits her natural talents. Sometimes it takes a little time and a little daydreaming to discover the right next step.

Tom's Story

Tom has been in supply chain and logistics for years in one form or another and enjoys the challenge. He knows how to move materials around a large system in an efficient, cost effective manner. It makes sense to him to continue in this profession because he can build on his experience and contacts. He can very specifically say he wants a position as a Supply Chain Manager.

What are your passions?

You've seen those cute slogans in Cracker Barrel, right?

> **"Recipe for Love."**
> Ingredients:
> 2 hearts full of love,
> 2 heaping cups of kindness, and
> 2 armfuls of gentleness...
> Method: Stir daily with happiness, humor and patience...

A little corny. But, the purpose is honest. Mix common elements to get a new result. Something to make you go "awww."

Can career change be like that? We meet people all the time who want something different. They work and work through unhappy days yearning for something different. What is the secret recipe for building a happy work experience?

Start with Passion.
Explore what makes you come alive. Passion is the fire inside us. Passion propels us to master difficulties. Passion energizes and inspires us. What is your passion? What activities have you encountered in your life that you still think about or that drove you through darkness?

Add a cupful of Dreams.
Your secret desires and longings. That place your mind goes when you let yourself relax. One theory says dreams are a way of practicing behavior or skills we need or crave. Where does your mind go when you relax? What activities, skills, behaviors are you curious about? What ideas do you explore when you read, watch TV, or wander through the Internet? The places you wander give insight into dreams.

Add an armful of Experience.
Was there some experience in your past you particularly enjoyed? Why? What was it that made the experience stimulating?

Stir in some Connections.
Who do you know who works in a job you find curious? Or, who has a skill you find intri-

guing, a skill that you have always dreamt about learning? Talk to those people. Do a lot of talking. What makes them happy? How do they pass the time? How did they end up in that career? Is it a career? Can a passionate person earn a living doing that?

Finally a dash of Energy.

A new direction should give you energy. You should feel a lift in your step when you think or talk about your passion and dreams.

Career change can be awesome and frightening. You know when you have found the right path at the place where passion, dreams, and energy collide with experience and connections. Something to make you go, "AH HA!"

Nia's Story

> *Nia loves sales. She loves figuring out how people work and how to get them to do what she wants them to do, an important skill among sales people and a skill that can carry over to other industries. Just about every business uses sales people to push their products and services into the marketplace so the possibilities are endless. Nia has an advantage in her search because she knows what she loves. The next step for her is to*

*figure out where to do it. That knowledge
will be core to her plan.*

Is there another path for you?
For years in my annual holiday letter, I talked
to my friends and family about my search for
"the next thing." I was in human resources for
years but I knew in my gut that I wanted to do
something else. My next job would not be Director or VP of Human Resources. I could not
yet define it but it wouldn't be the same thing I
had been doing for years. I wanted to step out
of corporate America and be my own boss. I
was tired of working at the whim of others. I
wanted to sink or swim on my own merits. I
just had no idea what "the next thing" would
be.

Is there a yearning in your soul for something different? Are you a closet entrepreneur
as I was? Are you ready to open a store or buy
a franchise? Do you want to "retire" and become a bus driver at Disney World? Or, maybe
like my husband, you want to become a tow-
boat captain on Lake Erie? This is your moment.

Exercises

In this portion of your plan, outline exactly what you are looking for in your next position. Use a separate sheet of paper to answer each of the following questions in detail.

- *In my next position, I want to be in this general field:*

_____

_____

_____

_____

_____

_____

_____

_____

_____

- *Doing this kind of work:*

Define who you are and What You Bring to the Table

Anthony's Story

> Anthony is a talented industrial engineer with an MBA from Purdue University. Unfortunately, he graduated with his MBA just after 9/11 when jobs were tight. Months after graduation he still did not have a job.

He was getting very frustrated. His parents were frustrated too. They wanted him to get started on his career, not hang around the house.

I could not figure out what the problem was. On the surface, he was the whole package. He was smart, educated, and personable. Perhaps the problem was the way he interviewed? So I asked some friends to interview him for a Production Manager position, something in his field. Turns out he was telling people he could do anything they wanted him to do. He was not being specific about what he brings to the table. He was hoping this made him more flexible. The longer he was out of work the more flexible he tried to be. Anthony was wrong.

Employers will not take any time to define you for you. Employers want to know what you want and who you are. Only with that information can they understand how you would fit into their organization.

You might think defining yourself too much will limit your possibilities. Not true. If you do some soul searching, there are some jobs you just will not do.

On the cable show, *Inside the Actor's Studio*, the host James Lipton, asks each actor a series of questions made famous by the French television personality Bernard Pivot. I always pause when he asks the ninth question, "What profession would you not like to do?" I find the answers fascinating.

The answers from actors range from Toll Booth Operator to Nurse and everything in between. Everyone has some limitations on the work they are willing to do.

I know what I would answer. I really do not enjoy recruiting. Ironic for someone who works with job seekers all the time, but it is true. Recruiting involves managing a lot of details and talking to lots of people. I would rather do almost anything than recruit. I even tried to talk someone out of giving me a consulting job involving recruiting. So if someone called me about a job recruiting, I would have to say no. I will not waste their time or my time pursuing something I really do not enjoy and probably will not be good at.

The kind of work you will and will not do forms a little island of possibilities for you to explore. This knowledge frees you up to deeply explore a smaller area rather than wasting your time pursuing jobs you know you would hate. This is a very important piece of information for your plan.

- **In my next position, I *DO NOT* want to do these kinds of jobs:**

_____

_____

_____

_____

_____

_____

_____

_____

I bet if you really think about it, you really love a particular field because it is work you are good at. The work you do not care for probably involves skills you are not good at. This is true in my case. I am not good with details. I am a 30,000 foot person. I have lots of ideas and I like to surround myself with detail-oriented people. I have to work very hard at budgets and finance. The other aspects of HR come much easier to me.

Perhaps it is the same with you. I suspect there are some aspects of the work you have been doing that you really love and parts you really dislike. It is probably related to your skills and interests. Your skills and interests are what you bring to the table; it is what you can offer to an employer.

It is critical that you understand what you bring to the table. Without a clear understanding of what you are, you will float around the job search like a balloon, going from one opportunity to another without knowing for sure whether anything in particular really fits.

Bill's Story

Bill loves his profession but hates his company. He knows what he is good at. Finance is his passion. He can point to clear accomplishments that support what he brings to the table. His issue is moving his skills and passion for finance to a workplace that values who he is and treats people well. This gives him a clear advantage over other job seekers who might be more muddled.

Defining who you are gives you some tangible basis to compare an open position to what is important to you. Otherwise, you might take the first job offered to you, which might make you very unhappy.

You will incorporate this information into your answers to interview questions so hiring managers know a little about you.

Since you will use this information in several ways during your job search, it is worth spending some time in the beginning to describe who you are.

- **I want this because I am:**

_____

_____

_____

_____

_____

_____

Here are a few critical questions to ask yourself to help define who you are. Write down your answers so you can reference this information in the future. You will come back to this many times as you prepare to interview and as you prepare to talk to other people about what you want and what you bring to the table.

- *Select five words to describe yourself.* These are words or short phrases that represent your values and strengths. Every person is different so everyone will select a different combination of words. For example, I think that I am smart, a team player, high energy, process oriented, and a problem solver. There is no right or wrong answers. The words you chose give insight into who you are and what you bring to the table. What are your five words?

1._____
_____
_____
_____
_____

2._____
_____
_____
_____
_____

3._____
_____
_____
_____
_____

4._____
_____
_____
_____

5._____
_____
_____
_____
_____

- *What attributes or skills make you different from other people.* These attributes or skills will be your selling point when you begin talking about yourself. For example, I understand business very well and love to solve problems in business organizations. What makes you different from other people who do the job you do?

On a separate sheet of paper, identify the attributes or skills that distinguish you from others.

- *What are your values?* Do you have a personal mission -statement reflecting your values? Your personal values and mission reflect what is most important to you and provides a basis for evaluating a potential job? For example, my personal mission is to solve people problems with humor and creativity so the organization thrives. I chose every word carefully. If a vacant position offered to me did not allow me to solve problems with humor and creativity, I would not be happy. I know I am not everyone's cup of tea. In the past I tried to make myself conform to environments where what I valued was not valued in return. I wasn't happy. You won't be happy in a position or an organization where you have to work outside of what is important to you either. So take some time in advance to work out the values most important to you.

On a separate sheet of paper, identify your core values.

I am different from others because...

_____

_____

_____

_____

Everyone is different. Human diversity adds to the complexity and depth of the workplace. You add value by defining why someone should hire you.

Ask yourself these questions about the qualities you possess:

- *I do this different or better than anyone else does...*

What are the things you do differently or better than anyone else? List them on a separate sheet of paper.

- *These are the good things that happen when or because I work...*

On your separate sheet of paper, list the positive outcomes that have resulted from your effort at work.

Your answers to these questions are based on your past experiences. Let me illustrate.

Katherine's Story

I am very strategic. I can put disparate information together and see patterns and potential solutions that others cannot see. This makes me different from other people doing the same job. It also makes me valuable to an organization that values strategic thinking. An organization that wants everyone to do exactly what they are told will not value my strategic thinking.

I need to find an organization that values the way I work and what is important to me. I do this by telling stories about my past experiences to illustrate the good things that happen when I am around.

I have many stories to describe the good things that happen when I strategically solve problems. I can use these stories to illustrate the value I bring to an organization without bragging. My past experiences also help illustrate to potential employers how I can fit in their workplace.

Sometimes the stories I tell eliminate me from consideration at companies that do not value my strengths. For this I say thank you! By defining who you are you help employers see how you can fit in, if you can fit in. It makes it easier to see which opportunities are right for you.

Let us consider Tom, our Supply Chain Manager. His five words are: *organized, detail oriented, quiet, smart, and passionate.* He loves to pull apart processes to figure out how to reduce costs. He can point to some big successes and has some great stories. He did not realize those stories were important. He thought he was just working and good things happened. But, those stories are critical. Writing down his answers to these critical questions along with stories about his successes made Tom feel more confident about what he has to offer.

Chapter 4

Is it my age?

The older version.

Tom's big concern was his age. Like many people, he thinks his age will knock him out of consideration for many companies who just want to hire young people. Interesting, many young people tell me they think companies only want to hire people with experience. So, many people at the younger and older end of the spectrum have similar concerns about their age.

Let's consider the question from the hiring managers' point of view. A hiring manager is looking for energy. Hiring managers are balancing four generations of workers on their teams. They are looking for vital, energetic, knowledgeable people who can solve problems and fit in with the rest of the team.

They are not interested in, and they do not have time to babysit, a cranky person who does not use, understand, or value, technology and who will not blend well with the rest of the team.

Into which group do you fit? If you want to find a job and you are an older person, you had better figure out how to demonstrate that you fit into the first category: that you are vital, energetic, and easy to work with. You must distinguish yourself from your cranky class-mates!

Easy to say but, you ask, how do I do that?

In an interesting article recently, Jesse Garza asked his readers "Are you stuck in a time warp?"[v] His theory is that people can get reluc-tant to change the comfortable vision of them-selves they cultivate when they are younger. But is precisely the change necessary to find a job in our modern workforce.

In my twenties, I took the Ravenswood El to work every day in Chicago. I stood on the platform in the morning with a woman who wore her hair in a bouffant style like the one you see in Grease. So, in the 1980s she wore her hair the same way she wore it when she was in high school in the 1950s. She was comfortable with herself. Anyone else would have thought she looked ridiculous.

If a woman dressed the same way she did in the 1980s wearing a suit with shoulder pads, a blouse with a string tie and big teased permed hair came to your office today for an interview, how would you react if you were the hiring manager? Most hiring managers would assume she was stuck in the past, not flexible, probably not technically savvy, and that she would probably not mesh well with the other people on the team. She would not make it past the first few minutes of the interview. She would not get the job. After a while, she would begin to think it was age discrimination.

Let's consider some ways to help this woman. Let's call her Gabriella. Let's also talk to her husband, Rick, also stuck in the 1970s in his approach to the world. Jess Garza has some very good ideas.

• **Embrace Technology**. Learn to text. Use Google instead of the yellow pages. If you need help, take a class or ask your kids.

• **Update Your Eyewear.** Old glasses make the wearer look old. If you are still wearing the style you wore in college, get a new pair of glasses. Go to an eyeglass store and ask a technician to help pick out a modern looking pair. It will feel awkward at first but go with it.

• **Get a Modern Haircut.** Invest in a makeover. Use hair color to cover your grey. Men, this applies to you too. You don't want to pretend to be twenty again but it is okay to look a few years younger than you are.

•   **Get a Second Opinion on Your Wardrobe.** Ask your kids for a frank review of your work clothes. Or go to a large department store and ask a sales person for some recommendations. Don't forget to think about your shoes.

•   **Go to the Gym.** The key is energy. You get energy and positive endorphins when you exercise. Exercise makes your skin glow and gives your muscles tone instead of flab. You don't have to look like a movie star. Regular exercise gives you the energy you need to demonstrate you will fit into a modern, four-generation workplace.

Jesse Garza puts it best: "As a Post-50 woman, when you walk into a room you want people to see the updated, modern, confident you, and not be distracted by all the bells and whistles of an era gone by, so get inspired, have fun, and reinvent yourself!"

The younger version.

James's Story

> *James is a senior at University of Illinois majoring in a high tech engineering field. He did everything right so far – he had good internships, he is working closely with his professors, he knows people at his target company, and he did a fascinating senior thesis that relates directly to his target position. In my view, he was not inexperienced. Yet he could not see himself as anything but an entry-level kid.*

James was undervaluing what he brings to the table. He already demonstrated he knows how to work and can point to demonstrated successes. He would add value immediately. It would be a shame if he sold himself short as an entry-level engineer. After talking it through, he started to see that employers place high value on what he offers. He went into the interview with much more confidence and nailed a full- fledged engineering position, not an entry-level role.

Young people have skills employers need and want. Again, consider it from the employers' point of view. As they balance four generations, they want employees who are vital, energetic, and work well with others. It is to your advantage to point this out to potential employers.

Chapter 5

Network: Know Where to Find It

You know what you want and why that is important to you. The next step of your plan is to find what you want.

We talk to many candidates who are frustrated because they feel like they have been working very hard at their job searches but nothing happens. They complain that employers do not call them back. They submit resume after resume but nothing happens. It seems unfair that you have to know someone to get a job.

Yes. Yes to all of it.

It is true that employers don't call candidates back.

It is true that if you just submit a resume, even hundreds of resumes, nothing happens. We had a client who could document submitting over 1000 resumes with only three callbacks.

It is true that you have to know someone to get a job. This is not necessarily a bad thing.

Human resource people tell stories of forwarding the first three to five resumes that come in to the hiring manager. If none of those resumes generates interest, they send the next five resumes. It might not be fair but do you really want to be stuck in this loop?

Submitting resumes is not effective. Ads are not a fraud. Employers who place job ads really want to add someone to their teams. They eventually will add someone to their team but the odds that your resume gets you the job are not in your favor.

Consider the odds: If 100 people submit their resumes in response to an ad, you are 1 in 100. There is little on a sheet of paper to really distinguish you from the 99 other people who applied. According to The Ladders, hiring managers spend about six seconds on each resume. So what are the chances your resume is the lucky one in 100 when there are so many resumes and yours only gets six seconds of review? The odds are not in your favor. We tell people this all the time but many, perhaps most job seekers are out there submitting resumes anyway. Their job searches take a long time.

To actually get a job you need to handle your job search in a manner that puts the odds in your favor.

Put your search energy where it can be most effective

Let's look at how effective various job search technique can be. Opinions vary and it is difficult to find exact studies on this topic. Some job search techniques are more effective than others are.

Submitting resumes: Success Rate – about 4%

Submitting resumes in response to ads found on Job Boards like Monster, Career Board, and other online posting boards is the least effective job search technique. This is the least personal, widest net a company can spread making it the least effective way for a candidate to find a job. The odds are not in your favor.

Email blasts to random employers: Success Rate –4 to 7%

This method is only slightly more effective because you might get lucky and send a random resume to a place that coincidentally is looking for someone like you. The odds are against you though.

Answering ads in professional trade journals or industry specific websites: Estimated Success Rate – about 7%

This method is slightly better because you are responding to an ad that is targeted to someone with your skills and experiences. Professional trade journals or industry specific websites do not attract the wide attention that job ads on job boards receive.

Answering local newspaper ads: Success Rate –7 to 12%

The higher end of this search method refers to responding to ads in online newspapers. This method is slightly more effective because the geography is close to home. Employers do not want to pay relocation so your local resume might get a little attention. Some people still answer ads posted in the printed newspaper. This method is not very effective and usually signals that the person is older since mostly older people read physical newspapers.

Employment agencies or search firms: Success Rate –5 to 28%

The success rate depends on the kind of job you are looking for. Employment agencies and recruiters usually specialize in certain kinds of jobs and have relationships with employers who have actual job openings. You are getting closer.

Networking for specific job leads from family, friends, community members, and alumni: Success Rate – about 33%

This method is significantly better than submitting random resumes. Make it even more effective by targeting your efforts to specific industries, companies, or people who can be helpful.

Knocking on doors of employers of interest: Success Rate – about 47%

This method is hard for shy people but shows employers you have courage and determination, characteristics welcome in many companies.

Conducting a career search in the unadvertised market by networking, researching, and reading business papers: Success Rate – about 69%

This method is so effective because time spent this way immerses you in the jobs and companies that are likely to hire you and in which you are likely to be happy.

Consulting with a team of career experts to make a job search plan and/or using a job hunting support group: Success Rate – about 84%

This method leverages people you know with people who know how to find a job. It is an investment in you.

Bottom line:

Least Effective: Answering ads
Most Effective: Networking

Networking and meeting people is the most effective way to find a job. It makes sense. There is a significant jump in effectiveness when networking is added to the formula. You get an added bump by leveraging your efforts with other people in a support group or using career experts.

These statistics are important whether you are looking for a job while currently employed or not. If you are currently employed and you want to work somewhere else, don't just answer ads. Odds are it will not work as well as networking.

If you are currently in college and preparing to find your next job, do not just answer ads. Get out there and meet people who can help with your search.

If networking is the best method of finding your next job, then organize each day and week focusing the majority of your time on networking in some way or another.

What is networking?
Networking is any effort you take that offers an opportunity to meet more people, talk to

more people who might be able to help you or to introduce you to more people. Getting a job is a question of numbers. The more people you talk to, the more opportunities you can find, the greater your chances of finding the job you love. It is a question of numbers.

You can be networking when you are using LinkedIn, setting up information interviews, meeting people for coffee and conversation, or just talking to people you know. The point is to get out there and talk to people to find the people who can help you.

Despite the clear evidence that networking is the most effective way to find your next job, many people avoid networking. We hear these kinds of excuses all the time:

- *The people I contact will not have a job for me to consider anyway*

- *The people I contact will not want to talk; people are SO busy*

- *Why should I take time to meet people now, I don't need a job*

- *If I do need a job, shouldn't I be filling out on-line applications?*

- *You don't understand. My industry is different. To get a job in my industry I have to answer ads in this journal only. I can't call them directly.*

Right? Wrong!!! Let's look at why saying 'NO' to networking is a mistake.

How often do you charge your cell phone? I plug mine in every night. If I don't pay attention and plug in my phone at night, or sometimes throughout the day, it will die. Your cell phone requires attention.

So does a job search. We use our phones all the time. We need our phones. We also need a job. We need to put as much effort and attention into energizing our job searches as we do in keeping our phones energized.

Networking and charging your phone have a lot in common. It's important to stay plugged in to a source of power that re-energizes you. That energy is contagious. Employers can sense candidates who are energized and engaged in their job search and those who are just going through the motions.

Here are five reasons to network:

1. Most jobs are filled by known to the recruiter – through networking. Surveys show that 65% - 75% of all jobs are filled through networking. Traditional meet-and-greet-and-build-friendship gatherings have not gone away. Moreover, social media is a form of networking. You can begin to make the connection with people through Facebook and LinkedIn and Twitter. Ultimately, though. . .

2. Networking gives you face-to-face meeting time. It's easier to see how someone would fit into an organization through a meeting rather than a resume. Getting in front of someone makes your resume personal. In those meetings, many times, you are interviewing for a job and you are not even aware of it. It may not be immediate but when an opportunity arises, you will be remembered and considered even though you have not applied.

3. Networking taps into "Six-Degree" wisdom. Through networking, you have the opportunity to speak with people you know and ask them to refer names of others that will benefit your search. Have you heard of the concept of 'Six Degrees of Separation? This concept refers to the idea that everyone is on average approximately six steps away, by way of introduction or association, from every other person on Earth, so that a chain of, "a friend of a friend" statements can be made, on average, to connect any two people in six steps or fewer. A friend of a friend may recommend someone who can offer you a job or open doors to others who can help you.

4. Networking teaches you how to fish. A recent Department of Labor report studied college-educated workers over a 30-year period from 1978 through 2008. The findings indicate that on average these individuals had between 10 and 11 different jobs in the course of their work lives. Will you change jobs again? The answer is probably, yes. Why not meet the people who can help you find your next job before you need that job?

5. Networking recharges you. The biggest natural attraction and reason for networking is the "re-chargeability" factor. You become the power behind your search. You take care to charge your cell phone every day. You can similarly take the responsibility for your career when you commit to networking. Networking is the event that recharges your self-worth and increases your positive energy concerning your work, whatever your work is today.

Getting your foot in the door.

Isabella's Story

> *Isabella is a professional healthcare administrator. She's a vice president at a hospital-based college, and is doing very well for herself. I remember when she started at that hospital. I worked in the department where*

Isabella worked as an unpaid, for-college-credit-only, intern. She established herself as someone we had to hire full-time. She stood out then, and she stands out now, some twenty-plus years later.

Isabella knew (by the choice of her major) that she wanted to work in human resources. She did not know that she wanted to work in a hospital. That just happened to be the organization that agreed to offer her an internship. She was by no means the only intern that came through our department in the five years I worked there. We did not hire every intern to a full-time position after their internship, although the majority did eventually work there full-time.

So what's the point of this internship success story? If you are a young person, wanting a good job when you receive whatever degree you are pursuing, how do you make that education work for you? How do you get your foot-in-the-door of an organization that will give you a chance, pay you well, and allow you to be a contributor?

If you are in a major at a college where internships are NOT part of your curriculum, know that the internship experience is an essential, must-have experience for you to get while pursuing your degree. It pains me to meet with college students (and I do regularly) whose primary goal seems to be to finish their program. If you have this mindset, and you will not have an internship experience when you graduate, you're making a mistake. Saving a few thousand tuition dollars and graduating without a relevant work experience is a dead-end!

Do you want a solid starter-job with a good work-environment when you graduate? (If you are farther along in your work life, and want a new career, this strategy can work for you, too!)

Then start talking to organizations who do work that intrigues you. If you talk to enough people about what you think you want to do, someone will offer you an internship experience. Take it! Build it into a job, or build it into a story that you can share with other organizations. Internship stories have gravitas in the workplace; hiring managers listen when you've done meaningful internship work while in school. It shows them that you offer relevance and value, and will be a contributor. It is the proverbial foot-in-the-door. Go get an internship now!

Where do you find this information?

Angela's Story

Angela, a college professor changing positions insisted that we did not understand. Jobs in colleges are filled through advertisements in a specific journal. However, she wasn't getting anywhere. So, we encouraged her to network, despite her skepticism.

She started meeting with people she met during her last assignment. One day she was having coffee with a couple of school administrators and got into a conversation about a problem they were having that fell into Angel's specialty area. She piped up with her experience and got their attention. By having coffee with the right people, she created an opportunity to show her stuff to people who can employ her. And, she did not have to file an application through that big journal. She goes to the head of the line of candidates because the people who matter already know her.

You only get this important information through research and social networking. You cannot find it in a book. You cannot obtain this advantage by submitting applications.

With all the information available on the Internet, there is no excuse for ignorance about people, companies, or entire industries. Invest some time on the computer as a start.

Begin with Google. Follow the path of the hundreds (or more) citations, reading to find the next string to follow. Then look up the company at investment sites like www.thestreet.com or www.morningstar.com. See how the financial world views the company. Follow the links for articles and press releases. Read 10Ks. Read industry journals and a business paper like Crain's to find articles about your target people, companies, and industries.

Use your imagination and be creative.

Anthony's Story

Anthony was interested in a position at a large distributor in Chicago area that is consolidating operations, a perfect opportunity for a logistics person. To get more information about this opportunity he Googled the company name and followed the links to learn about new initiatives, promotions, and news. With this method, he learned about that the company had de-centralized divisions and was thinking about consolidation. By doing this research, he was able to talk intelligently about ways to take advantage of cost reductions and synergy. His research impressed the folks he networked with. He did not get the open position. Instead, they brought him on board as special project leader for the consolidation reporting to the President. All because he did research and networked.

☐

Chapter 6

Social Networking

Social networking adds new research possibilities.

Let's look at this from the company's perspective. When a company seeks to add someone to their team, they spread a net to find candidates. They might advertise, they look for referrals from their employees and friends, and these days they look around social networks to find people who might meet their requirements, whether those folks are looking for work right now or not.

So, if you are looking for a new position, one strategy is to place yourself in the line of sight of employers who might be looking to add folks to their teams. You want to land in their net. You do this through networking.

These days networking takes at least two forms. The traditional method is still effective.

You reach out to talk and meet people through people you know in person (phone calls, meetings, and letters). You must also reach out virtually through social networking.

Young people use social networking all the time. It is the way they communicate with each other. I am talking about Facebook, texting, Twitter, Flickr, Google Plus, and a myriad of other means. Business people use Linkedin.com to meet people, exchange information, and generally network.

If you are not familiar with some or all of these ways to network, then you are not taking advantage of all the ways you can put yourself in the line of sight of people who are hiring. In other words, your job search is (or will soon be) stalled.

I use Facebook to keep in touch with friends and family, text my kids, email constantly, Flickr and Picasa for pictures, and Linkedin.com for business networking.

My husband thinks it is all a bunch of hooey and constantly gripes that people should just pick up the phone and talk. He has a point, but sticking strongly to his point means he misses the boat in communicating with as many people as he can in a job search. Thank goodness he is not conducting a job search or he would be stuck.

I use Linkedin.com more than any social networking tools to expand my contacts, meet people, research companies, and get the word out about my areas of interest. You should too.

LinkedIn *offers great networking opportunities*

Here are some tips to get the most out of LinkedIn:

• **Complete your profile to 100%.** This is a top priority. Recruiters and employers don't even look at profiles that are not 100% completed. Make sure your profile includes lots of accomplishments and summarizes your goals, just like your resume so your profile makes a good impression.

• **Add a professional looking picture.** Many people avoid this but it is critical. Your profile can't be 100% complete without a picture. Do not use a picture of you at a party laughing and holding a beer. Make it a professional picture. If you do not have one, seriously consider visiting a professional photographer to get a good picture. Make sure you look friendly and nice. No grimaces or frowns allowed!

• **List all your former employers and schools for maximum reach.** When you extend an invitation to connect, you will be asked how you know this person. Listing your former employers and schools you attended makes it easier to say that you know someone as a former colleague or classmate. Otherwise, you must provide an email address. It makes it easier to send invitations if you can honestly say you know the person through a former employer or school.

• **Ask for recommendations** from people you worked with. They will respond by asking you to return the favor so be sure you can say something nice about them too.

• **Find contacts.** Use the automated contact-finder built into Linkedin.com to search your telephone directory and email for contacts then invite those people to connect with you on Linkin.com. Look through your written telephone directory and search for people you know by using the "people" search at the top right side of your profile. I used to be shy about asking for connections because I wasn't sure how people would respond to me. I stopped worrying about this and you should too.

• **When people send you invitations to connect, accept!** Don't look at those folks as strangers. Look at them as people you are meeting for the first time.

• **Connect with your connections' connections.** When you connect with someone, look through their contacts to see who you know then send them an invitation to connect.

• **Join groups.** What are your interests? Start with a focus on groups related to the work you do. There are usually several. For example, as an HR person, I joined groups related to our professional group, SHRM, local and national HR interest groups, subgroups related to specialties like organizational development, talent, or recruiting. Look at the members tab to see who you might know.

• **Expand into groups** related to your industry or the industries you want to work in. I worked in building materials distribution so I joined groups related to building materials, distribution, supply chain, and sales.

• **Join your alumni association group.** There might be several of those too if you went to a large school. Then look for people you knew in college and ask them to connect. Recently I found a friend from college I lost touch with years ago. Turns out he works in training and had, as a client, one of my company's large vendors. We had a nice chat and now stay in touch. I am confident that if I needed help I could call on him for advice.

- **Get involved.** Look around the groups and see what they are talking about. Join a few conversations. Sometimes that gets you introduced to more people who have similar or different views. Recently I responded to a conversation that led to an introduction and a referral to more interesting people.

Bill's Story

> Bill had never done any social networking other than the usual Facebook stuff. A while ago, he opened a LinkedIn account but did not really have a profile and had only about five contacts. Since he wanted to change jobs while working, he was concerned that completing his profile and adding contacts would draw unwanted attention from his boss, the jerk. We assured him to do it anyway.

We advised him to create a story in case anyone noticed. He decided he would tell people who noticed his increased networking that he was looking for new ideas about a particular project and figured out that LinkedIn Groups would be a great way to talk to other people to get ideas.

Bill proceeded to complete his profile over the weekend and started sending out invitations to connect. He joined groups about finance and made sure those groups were visible on his profile. He joined job seeker groups and made sure those groups were private on his profile. He joined his local professional group and attended regularly. He started meeting people who could help his search.

Best of all, his boss never noticed his increased LinkedIn activity! His search continued under the radar screen and he brought new ideas back to work that enhanced his reputation in his current job. It did not however change his boss!

Best practice about contacts.

When someone sends you an invitation or accepts your invitation, do not just let it drop. Accept the invitation then say thank you. In the Inbox tab, send the new contact a note that says it is great to connect with him or her. Check out their profile and find something interesting. Then in your note say something about his or her profile.

Once after I started doing this, I got a request to connect from Theresa in human resources at a local accounting firm. I checked out her profile and noticed she is a scuba diver. I also scuba dive. So I sent her a note asking where she dove recently? She responded and we had a little email exchange about scuba diving that led to a meeting and eventually to some consulting work. I could have also called her on the phone after the email exchange.

The best practice is to follow up with a note and/or a phone call to build a relationship. After all, the point is not to rack up lots of contacts. The point is to build a networking base of contacts you can help and who can help you in return. In other words, build relationships.

The best practice in sending invitations is to send a little note indicating who you are and how they know you. LinkedIn provides standard language in the message. Everyone uses that. Only a few take the time and show the initiative to make a comment in addition to the standard supplied language. Your note could look something like this:

> *Ethan, I enjoyed our conversation at the Chamber of Commerce meeting yesterday. I would like to connect with you on LinkedIn to see how we can help each other.*

Your connection request will get an extra look, guaranteed. You will demonstrate you are different from the average LinkedIn user.

If you are a job seeker expanding your network, each time you respond with a comment, a note, or a thank you that is beyond the minimum, you open the door for further conversations and networking. Just imagine the possibilities!

After all, LinkedIn is about networking, and networking is about building rapport. Rapport leads to meetings that lead to more contacts and eventually to the right person who can extend to you a great job offer. So pay attention to the little things like starting conversations with new contacts. It is a great way to network.

LinkedIn Groups

LinkedIn groups are particularly useful to research companies. LinkedIn Groups are your networking key to the kingdom. Groups give you access to even more people, more information about companies, job opportunities, and exposure.

Let's look at some ways Groups can help:

• **Expands your Contacts.** LinkedIn protocol allows you to send an invitation to connect with people who are in groups with you without knowing their email address. Being in groups allows you to connect with more people and allows other people in the group to connect with you.

• **Interesting Discussions.** You can post questions or add comments to questions other people post. This raises your visibility and lets people see how you think. Assuming you make a good impression, it makes you more desirable.

• **Jobs.** Jobs are posted in Groups that might not be visible anywhere else. You can respond directly and perhaps get a leg up on the competition. You might also become aware of companies hiring people in your field.

• **Increases your visibility.** The more people who know you are looking, the more likely you can land that job. Recruiters use LinkedIn as their top choice to find candidates. They look in groups. If you are not there, they won't find you!

• **More ways to search for people, companies, and jobs.** Motivational speaker Tom Krause said, "If you only do what you know you can do, you never do very much." If you only network with people you already know, you won't get very far. Groups offer you the chance to get outside of your circle to meet people, learn things, and find opportunities outside of your small circle.

Join groups related to your education (college alumni association, college interest groups, sorority or fraternity groups), your previous employment, special interest groups related to your job, groups related to your industry or the industry you want to work in, special interest groups related to some special characteristic about you (maybe your age, sex, race). Be careful about groups related to your religion or politics so you don't inadvertently alienate potential employers. LinkedIn groups are a must in every job search.

Consider the impact of thoughtful opinions.
A while ago I joined a group called Transformational Leadership. I like to think that I am a transformational leader so I thought it would be fun. The first discussion I saw was a group of folks complaining that the people at Occupy Wall Street should work through the system instead of protesting. I thought it was odd that people who thought they were transformational leaders would object to an activity that wants to transform or change the status quo. So I made a comment to that effect. Within hours I sparked a new discussion and connected with several really thoughtful leaders.

I would never have had that experience or gotten those connections if I had not stepped out of my circle into a new group. I do not know yet how these connections will affect me or benefit me in the future but I bet someday they will. Isn't that what networking is all about?

What is the right number of contacts?

Having more LinkedIn contacts allows you to leverage to your contacts' contacts, those people who are connected to the people you know. The more contacts you have, the more people you know, the more people you can access through other people. A job seeker should have at least 100 contacts in order to have any leverage.

As a big LinkedIn fan, I always encourage job seekers to expand their presence on LinkedIn. You can't imagine the number of times I have heard people say, "I get invitations to connect all the time but I only accept those from people I know very well."

I find this view annoying. Let's imagine this attitude from a different point of view. Let's say you go to a cocktail party and only talk to the people you know already. There will be little clumps of people all over the room but no mingling. How would you learn anything new or get a different perspective?

Or, imagine you go to a business meeting of people in your company from different parts of the business. You stand like a lump next to the only other person you know while everyone else mingles. You wouldn't want to meet someone you don't already know, right?

When I was young, I was very shy. My first husband was quite outgoing and had a job that required that he and his wife (me) be very social. It was torture to go into a room full of people I did not know. To overcome this problem, I forced myself to talk to at least three people I did not know before I slunk back to my corner with my friends. You know what? After a while, I realized I enjoyed meeting people. I ask lots of questions to get the other person to talk. Curiosity overcame my shyness.

LinkedIn is a wonderful way for shy people to step out. No one can see you. You are safe.

There are lots of reasons to meet people you don't already know in the real world or in the social network that is LinkedIn.

1. People you don't know might be able to answer a question you have. You could learn something.

2. They know people you need to know. Imagine the difference between submitting your resume to an advertisement or sending your resume to a person you know. Which resume is the hiring manager going to look at?

3. They know something about a company you are researching. Wouldn't it be nice to call someone you know and ask questions?

4. You can have an interesting conversation with them on a discussion page, raising your visibility and encouraging recruiters to look at your profile.

5. Networking is about connecting to people you don't know yet. Why wouldn't you accept an invitation or reach out?

Don't be shy. Reach out and link with someone! Activate your job search using social networking.

Take active steps to identify companies that make sense for you.

You know who you are and what you want. Now you can identify a few companies that make sense for you. Taking this active step gives you control over your job search. Google and Research USA are good sources for this information. Most companies have LinkedIn or Facebook sites with lots of company information. Don't ignore the information readily available on social networking. You can also use sites like www.GlassDoor.com to see what some employees think about your target company. Temper what you read on that site because unhappy people are most motivated to post on GlassDoor. You are not hearing a balanced view. But it can be useful information.

Tom's Story

Tom, the supply chain manager, has experience with plastics companies. He identifies five or six different companies in the plastics and related fields where he can apply his previous experience. Some of them are competitors so he knows them pretty well already. He researches these companies to see which organizations would be most comfortable for his values and style. During his research, he identifies people he knows who work at those companies and other people he would like to meet. This gives him a way to begin networking.

He sends LinkedIn invitations to connect with those he knows. He joins some industry groups and is able to connect easily with people he does not yet know but who can be helpful. He personalizes the invitations and follows up later to arrange coffee to build relationships. In this way, he turns the contact into someone who can actually help him. He gets referrals to more people in other companies. He joins a job seekers group and his local professional group and meets even more people.

His Job Search Marketing Plan is working! He is meeting people who can help, learning about new companies, and finding out about opportunities before they are posted as job openings.

Contract Work.

What happens if you are seeking a new position but you already left your last position? Many employers prefer to hire people who are currently employed. After a giant recession like that experienced in 2007 to early 2010s, it seems unfair and downright short-sited to exclude folks who are not currently employed but some employers view candidates not currently employed as somehow damaged. This point of view adds insult to injury to an out of work job seeker.

Contract work and consulting provide good cover if you are currently out of work as well as providing necessary family income while you wait for the right permanent job.

Find contract work in somewhat the same way you find a regular job. Here are some options:

• **Temporary agencies** often have positions for professional workers, especially staff positions like finance, accounting, human resources, information technology, and engineering. Find agencies by Googling in your local metropolitan area.

• **Network with friends and contacts** to see if anyone has a need for your services on a temporary basis.

• **Ask your former employer** (if you left on good terms) or contractors if they have a need for someone to do some temporary work.

• **Some skills offer the opportunity to market your services to businesses** in your area by posting notices in local supermarkets and coffee shops. For example, graphic designers and computer experts can generate some income by a bit of local advertising.

• **Craigslist** is a good place to advertise for people or companies who might need your services on a contract or consulting basis.

Charlie's Story

Charlie was a sales person specializing in software and medical devices before losing his job in a layoff. Early in his career, he did some consulting for his family business setting up their networking computer system. To appear to be employed and to bring in income while he waited he started doing small computer consulting projects. He changed his resume to reflect that he opened his own consulting practice after leaving his last job. When asked, he can now say he is currently employed but is open to opportunities in the corporate world. It is no one's business but his that he never really intends to stay in the consulting business.

Using Recruiters.

Recruiters can be another source of contacts and leads so some positions. Many times recruiters will find you, usually through LinkedIn if your profile is 100% complete. Or, maybe a friend gives you a recruiter's name. Recruiters look at the work in a different way. They have a different perspective.

Here are a few tips from a recruiter's perspective – when to use a recruiter, what to expect (and not expect), what to ask, and how to maximize this potential job-seeking aide:

• **Consider a recruiter only if you have worked at least five years:** If you are relatively new to your profession, it's not as likely you'll find recruiters helpful. With the ease of the internet at the fingertips of all, including hiring managers, employers themselves typically fill junior-level positions.

• **Stay employed:** Hiring managers today seem to have a strong bias toward candidates who are already employed, so make your connection while you are still employed, if possible. If you are out of work, or underemployed, you'll need a good story, and may want to consider employing yourself.

• **Determine whether to call the company first or the recruiter:** If you're interested in a particular company, and you've networked to a decision-maker, go directly to the company. If you don't know anyone at the company, and you talk with a recruiter who does have a personal relationship with the company and/or a hiring manager, utilize that relationship, and go through the recruiter.

• **Target your niche recruiters, and cultivate.** Begin by identifying niche recruiter agencies that specialize in the types of jobs, the industries, and the areas of the country where you would like to work. Check the niche agency job postings on their website often, and when your experience fits a job well that is posted, pursue an acquaintance with someone in that agency. 'I match the requirements well to a job you have posted' is a good tactic to begin a productive conversation with a recruiter.

• **Make yourself 'findable':** Keep your online profiles (LinkedIn, Monster, CareerBuilder, etc.) up to date, and use as many 'keywords' in your niche as possible. You can add key words as you hear of positions that sound interesting. Recruiters look for candidates on these sites.

- **Recruiters find people for jobs (not jobs for people):** Although at times recruiters may offer to tweak your resume or suggest some interviewing tips, do not mistake the recruiter for your agent. Recruiters are paid by the client, and will take care of the client; that's who's paying them for their services.

- **Communication with a recruiter may be helpful:** Recruiters can provide you good information about what they see in the market place in a particular industry or type of job. They may (or may not) be courteous, generous in providing useful information, or prompt in getting back to you. Let me say it again: remember how the recruiter is paid – when they fill a job; that's what drives a recruiter's interactions with you.

- **Make the recruiter your friend.** Try throwing the recruiter some business. Offer an introduction to somebody within your network who's also looking and who would welcome contact with a recruiter. The recruiter may return the favor by keeping you in mind for future jobs.

- **Approach a recruiter like it's a game of poker.** You want to appear confident, poised, and with a bit of panache. Be aggressive and strategic, not intent on answering every job posting you can find. If you respond to jobs to which you are marginally qualified, you are creating a bad impression. A sense of desperation is a turn-off to recruiters, leery of wasting time on someone who already turned down by a bunch of companies.

Questions to ask a recruiter who calls you about a job?

- **What are the job requirements?** Ask for a job description, or a copy of the job posting.

- **What company?** They may or may not be willing to tell you at first ('confidential search'); however, if you have already applied to the company, or another recruiter has presented you there, you want to know, so you can control the situation. Candidates submitted by multiple sources often get eliminated (refereeing turf wars do not appeal to employers.)

- **What is the salary range?** If the recruiter asks first, be honest and up front about your own current salary, and what you would be willing to consider. If the job's defined range and your salary requirements are too far apart, you'd be wasting your time and that of the recruiter. (If you are currently unemployed or underemployed, it's an altogether different strategy. However much information you choose to share, always be honest.)

• **What is the history of this position?** If a replacement, what happened to the person who left? How long has is it been open? If it is a new position, how and why was it created?

• **What is the timetable?** What steps are involved in the hiring process? How soon will I hear back? When would they like someone to start?

• **How many other candidates are you representing to this client?** And, are there other agencies involved in the search?

• **The qualifier question:** Is there anything I said that would keep you from recommending me?

If handled correctly, recruiters are a resource and a potential avenue. Know how to approach them, and when; they may be the answer to finding your next interesting position.

Jessica's Story

Jessica is a good candidate for a recruiter. She has about five years of sales experience. She can now explain how her sales experience in selling to senior citizens can apply to other fields. She completes her LinkedIn profile to 100% and joins several groups in which she sees that recruiters are active. Soon she is getting calls from recruiters for sales jobs in medical supplies just as she wanted. Her Job Search Marketing Plan is working!

You know what you want and you have an idea where to find it. You identified people to talk to by your research and expanding your LinkedIn contacts. Now what? Now you get out there and talk to people through informational and networking interviews. Or, as we like to say, go have coffee.

Chapter 7

Informational and Networking Interviews.

A great way to get information about careers and jobs is to ask people who already do that job or who already work in a company in which you have interest. Just reach out and ask people. Here are some ways these kinds of meetings are different from a job interview.

- You request and schedule a networking or informational interview.

- You get names of people to call from referrals, generally.

- These are short interviews, usually less than 30 minutes.

- You come prepared with questions you would like to know about a particular job or company.

- You listen more than you talk; your part of the interview is asking follow-up questions.

Informational Interviews are meetings you organize with people who have information you want to know about companies, professionals, and business ideas. Anyone can set up an informational interview.

Successful Informational Interviews

If you look up "Informational Interview" in Wikipedia, here's what you get: "a meeting in which a job seeker asks for career and industry advice rather than employment. The job seeker uses the interview to (ask the questions), gather information on the field, and expand their professional network. This differs from a job interview because the job seeker asks the questions."

Here are some tips on organizing an informational interview over coffee. It helps to have a script in front of you when you make this phone call so you sound professional.

> *Hi, this is Tom. Paul suggested I give you a call because you are such an expert on Supply Chain at QRS Company. I was wondering if you have about twenty minutes next week to share your thoughts on this field. I know you are busy. I promise it will just take twenty minutes and I will buy the cof-*

fee. Great! How about Java Joe's at the corner of State and High Streets at ten A.M. on Wednesday? ..... Wonderful. I look forward to talking with you then.

Okay, so what questions should you ask when you do an informational interview well. Here are my top ten:

1. What is the job like day to day? What do you do in a typical day? What have you done over this past week or couple of days?

2. Hone in on expected talents. What are the key skills expected in their job? For example, a nurse needs to be able to assess patients, record what observations in a document, etc.

3. How did you learn those skills? On-the-job? In a classroom? Internship? From an informal mentor(s) when they started? How did they get the experience needed? Do you enjoy what you do? What drew you to this work? A paycheck? A friend? A relative? A teacher? What challenges do you face day-to-day and how do you tackle them?

4. What is it like to work for this company? What do you like? What do you dislike? How does the company compare with competitors in the industry?

5. What is your role in this job? How does your role contribute to this company? Are you a revenue generator, one of the doers, part of an infrastructure support team, a strategic implementer? How do you fit in to the big picture?

6. How do you view the work in this industry? Is it innovative? Could we do a quick mini- SWOT (Strengths, Weaknesses, Opportunities, and Threats) analysis of the industry, employment opportunities, education required.

7. Is my target position a new kind of role or it is a traditional role? For example: an intervention specialist in the field of education is a relatively new position. They develop independent action plans for at-risk students. Ten years ago, this position did not exist, and now it is one of the fastest growing areas.

8. Where are the job opportunities in your area? They will be different given the career opportunity you are considering: sales professional, accountant, IT professional, teacher, CNC operator, and manufacturing engineer. Knowing what kinds of companies or organizations are hiring may help you identify opportunities based on company size, and help determine whether you should look for em-

ployment in a large metro area or a medium-to-smaller community.

9. What are your personal job experiences and how were you hired? People like to talk about themselves, once they know you really care what they have to say. Put them on a bit of a pedestal, and feel the love.

10. What else do I need to do to land a position in your industry? Many times, they will be able to tell you what training is needed, and what can be learned on the job.

Remember to ask follow-up questions. Preparation gives your curiosity an edge. Be as prepared as you can about what they do. Link your curiosity to asking follow up questions as they say things about which you want to know more. When something peaks your interest it will help steer the conversation. This is meant to be a dialogue or interaction, not an interrogation.

Ask difficult questions that you can't easily find on the Internet. For example, if you are new to teaching and talking to an experienced teacher, don't ask about things you should already know, like lesson plans or classroom management. Ask hard questions. Aren't kids kind of crazy some times? Or parents? Or administrators? How do you handle difficult students? What has been your experience with No Child Left Behind or teaching to standardize testing?

Don't waste your contact's time. Make the most of your time in an informational interview to obtain information you can't get from a book or the Internet.

Jessica's Story

Since Jessica wants to get a sales job in a new industry, she needs to understand better which industry is right for her. After all, there is a big difference between selling pharmaceuticals and selling medical supplies. She needs to understand the difference so she can speak intelligently to people in that industry.

She leverages her new LinkedIn contacts to ask for some informational interviews from people who work in pharmaceuticals and in medical supplies. She makes the calls and to her surprise, almost everyone she calls agrees to speak with her. This means lots of coffee.

After several discussions she decides that medical supplies is better for her because it offers the best use of her skills and interests and it sound like it is easier to make the transition. She would not have known this if she did not ask for information.

Knowledge is power, and the more you know about a potential job option, the more powerful your perspective will be, all from good questions, and then listening to your contacts talk.

Keep the interview to exactly the amount of time you requested. It is only polite. Your goal is to have a conversation that builds a relationship. Your final questions are always, "Who else do you suggest I speak to?" This is a great way to add more contacts and meet more people.

Since looking for a new job is a question of numbers, the more people you know, the shorter your job search will be. Informational interviews are a good way to expand your contacts and get information at the same time.

If you do this right, informational interviews will help you determine if this type of job or this type of work is something you would want to do.

Networking interviews are slightly different from Informational Interviews. With Informational interviews, you are seeking information about a field, career, and company. Networking interviews are a way to obtain information about a company or about other contacts who can introduce you to people who can advance your job search.

Consider the differences and similarities between networking and informational interviews.

Similarities

- Both are called by the candidate
- Both should be short
- Send thank you notes after each
- You ask questions.
- Listen more than talk.
- Both build relationships with new people.

Differences

- You already know what career you want
- Networking interviews are designed to solicit contacts or leads on particular jobs
- Informational interviews are a good place to brainstorm with knowledgeable people about your career.

Anyone can be a good networking interview target. Personal friends, LinkedIn contacts, former colleagues, former classmates, old bosses and co-workers, people you meet socially or in your neighborhood. The possibilities are endless.

Make contact through any means you can: email, telephone, or in person. I like to make my initial contact by email, text, or through LinkedIn because I am shy about talking on the phone. My partner is more outgoing and loves talking on the phone so he starts with a telephone call. Whichever way is more comfortable for you. It also matters which method your contact prefers. If you send an email and get no response, try a phone call or text message. The point is to be persistent until you are able to make contact.

Tips for requesting a network interview:
You request a networking interview in almost the same way you request an informational interview. The wording changes slightly.

- Ask for a few minutes of your contact's time.

- Be prepared to suggest a place to meet. Sometimes you must meet on Skype if the person travels frequently or is out of town. Practice ahead of time so you can manage the technical aspects of the method you choose.

- It sometimes works better to have a referral. It is easier to get an appointment when you can say, "Anthony Smith suggested I contact you while I am networking."

- Have a reason why you want to speak to the contact. It can be related to a meeting you recently attended, an article the person wrote recently, something special going on in their company that you would like to leverage into a conversation, changes in the business field related to your specialty. The point is to have a reason to call. It can be as simple as networking to meet someone from ABC Company as you network in your job search.

Tips for conducting a networking interview:
Your goal in a networking interview is to get more names of people to talk to and to get information about a specific company or lead.

- Prepare questions in advance so you look organized and don't waste precious time.

- Take notes.

- Research the company and the person. Look the person and company up on LinkedIn and Google them so you know something about them.

- Arrive on time.

- Smile and have a good handshake.

- Dress appropriately, as if it were a job interview. It might turn into one if you play your cards right!

- Ask for a business card.

- Have your own business card and offer it at the beginning of the meeting.

- Say thank you at the end. Send thank you note immediately afterwards.

- Don't forget to ask if the contact can recommend someone else to speak to. Remember the purpose of the meeting is to make a good impression and to be introduced to more people to widen your network and increase your visibility.

Bill's Story

Bill joins the local finance professional group and starts meeting people in other companies. He calls Joe at ABC Company to network. He makes an appointment for coffee after the next meeting. Terrence has some insight into changes in the finance department at ABC Company and suggests Bill talk to Alyssa, the VP Finance. Bill and Alyssa connect and talk about ABC Company's project to implement SAP for the back office. Turns out Bill just implemented SAP at his company last year and has some good ideas about how to avoid potential problems. Alyssa is impressed and wants Bill to talk to Sofia in IT. After several more meetings and a bit of time, Bill gets an offer from Alyssa for a Financial Manager position with a critical role in the SAP implementation. This is exactly the role Bill wants in a company where people respect each other. He thinks he can work well with Alyssa and already likes Terrence.

Bill's Job Search Marketing Plan gave him the roadmap to use his time effectively while still working to meet the people who helped him find the new job he loves. His former boss is still a jerk but has to find someone new to kick around!

Chapter 8

Devise a Plan of Action

Commitments you make to yourself

You know what you want. You have a good idea about where you can find it. Since a job search is a numbers game, the more people you meet, the sooner your job search will be over. The more time you devote to your job search the faster you will get a job. Couple the numbers game with the knowledge that most people get a job from networking, you get an idea how to divide your time.

Since networking is the most effective method of obtaining your next job, you know you should spend the majority of your time on networking. The trick is figuring out how to do spend your time.

Structure your day around actions that support the cause

Sometimes you choose when to change jobs and sometimes the time chooses you. You might be changing jobs while still working at another job or you might be laid off with lots of time to devote to your job search. Both situations present time management challenges.

How do you structure your day? Where to begin? How do you spend your time?
If you are not working, this is not the time to take a vacation or clean out your closets. Well maybe a little cleaning can be therapeutic. But, this is a great time to clear the decks and focus most of your attention on your search.

If you are working, you must identify time every week to devote to your job search. If the change is important to you, you will figure out how to make this happen. Perhaps you devote the first thirty minutes in the morning and after lunch to networking on LinkedIn. You can make networking appointments for lunch or coffee after work. Begin attending your industry or professional association and make connections. You don't have to shout from the top of your lungs that you are looking for a new job. But, there are ways to make your interests clear.

First priority for any job seeker is to *create a Roadmap.* This can take some time but without a roadmap, you might wander around longer than Moses did.

1. Figure out what you want to do. Do you want to keep doing the same job you have been doing? Fine. At least that is a decision. Do you want to do something different? Plan it out.

2. Where you can do that? What companies have jobs like that?

3. Who should you network with to make it happen?

Once you have a plan, you need to implement. How do you structure your day while you work your plan? As a veteran job seeker, I have some ideas about how to structure your laid-off-days. Use the 80/20 rule:

**80% of your time on your job search
20% of your time on personal activities**

Why personal activities? Because all work and no play makes a dull job seeker. Personal activities could include walking the dog, exercising, cleaning those closets, working on a project in the garage, yard work or anything else you love to do.

Let's break down that 80% of time spent on job search a little more.

We can apply the 80/20 rule to this portion too:

**80% to 90% of your time networking
10% to 20% of your time answering ads**

Networking includes meeting people who work at your target companies or work in the field you want, LinkedIn networking, and coffee meetings with people you meet, attending professional association meetings, volunteering in some fashion in the field in which you want to work or in the community.

Every job seeker should have a LinkedIn profile at 100%, have at least 100 LinkedIn contacts and be involved in at least 6 groups. We consider it networking when you add contacts and participate in discussions with LinkedIn groups. This increases your visibility and moves your job search forward. Set a goal to add a certain number of LinkedIn contacts every week.

If you are working, you might be afraid that upgrading your LinkedIn profile might draw attention. If someone at work asks why you are spending time on LinkedIn, talk about how much you are learning about your current job from people on LinkedIn. You are learning so much and getting new ideas from the people you meet. This is your story and you are sticking to it.

Do not spend more than 20% of your job search time answering ads. I do not care if you think your industry is different. Most successful candidates obtain their job through networking so despite your beliefs, put your time into networking and minimize answering ads. Don't stop answering ads. Just don't spend the bulk of your time on ads.

Tom's Story

Tom found that having a plan helped structure his time while he was laid off. He was used to structure and liked it. He was a morning person so every morning he spent 30 minutes to an hour working on LinkedIn – expanding contacts, following and participating in conversations in groups, and checking out new positions posted in groups. He scheduled coffee for networking between ten A.M. and two P.M.

In the afternoon several times a week, he went to the gym. He picked up his daughter after high school and took her to soccer practice after school. In the evening, he sent out thank you notes and followed up on leads from earlier networking meetings. This schedule kept him balanced 80% on job search and 20% on personal. Within his job search time he made sure he spent at least 80% of his time on networking. He marks his progress on a detailed project plan that reflects the steps he plans to take to get the job he wants.

He met lots more people who could be useful in his search. During a job seekers club meeting, he heard that QBG Company was looking for a Director Supply Chain and Logistics. He did not know anyone who worked at QBG himself so he checked his contacts at LinkedIn. Turns out a colleague he worked with several years ago is a first level connection to someone at QBG. He contacted that person and got an invitation to connect with the VP Finance. That person gave him helpful information about the company and was very impressed with Tom's resourcefulness and background. He parlayed that connection into a meeting with the VP of Logistics.

These relationships got Tom to the top of the pile, resulting in an interview for the Director of Supply Chain and Logistics. He called The Interview Doctor for help preparing for the interview. He nailed the interview and got the job!

The Job Search Marketing Plan worked!

Get out there and meet people to move your job search forward!

Getting Something Done.
We all have only twenty-four hours in a day. How you use those twenty-four hours makes a difference.

- *Can you say you accomplished something every day?*

- *Are you moving the needle towards your goal?*

- *What else could you be doing?*

Christopher's Story

Christopher had been an athlete his entire life. An injury changed his plans. Now he was a job seeker, not a professional athlete. He struggled with how to spend his time.

As an athlete, he said he knew what he needed to do every day. He knew that not every ball he shot would go into the basket. Although, he knew that if he practiced, the odds increased that he would make a basket.

Why could we not transfer that lifelong discipline to his job search? As soon as we started talking about the job search as a disciple that could be practiced, his face lit up and he felt more comfortable.

Here are some ideas about how to manage your time to achieve your goals:

1. Set goals. Each day know what you want to accomplish. Exactly what you want to accomplish is up to you. However, without a goal, you won't get anywhere.

2. **Follow up.** Maybe your goal for Tuesday is to contact five people to set up information interviews. You make the calls but only reach two people. You leave voice mails with the other three people. The next day your goal should be to follow up with the three people, along with anything else you want to accomplish.

3. **Know what you want.** If you are looking for a job in banking, focus on banking. Stay focused. Don't wander all over because the truth is, if you want to work in banking you probably won't want to work in a factory. So focus on banking and stay away from distractions. Unless you decide that your focus is changing. Then put your energy behind your new focus.

4. **Be realistic about what you can accomplish in the day or planning period.** Is it realistic to think you can make twenty calls in one day? I couldn't, but maybe you can. I changed my planning process a few years ago to plan for a week because I was consistently unrealistic about what I needed/could accomplish in a day.

5. **Give yourself a break if you don't finish absolutely everything on your list.** It happens. Maybe you weren't realistic. Put those tasks on your plan for the next day.

6. **Plan time for yourself** – exercise, relaxation, time with friends and family. You need energy that comes from recharging. Plan it in your schedule so you are sure it happens.

Since this is a numbers game, consider using daily and weekly schedules to help you become more disciplined. These lists give you a sense of accomplishment as you look back over the day or week.

What are you willing to do to get a job?

A job search is a numbers game. The more people you know, the more companies you talk to, the wider you're net, the faster you will find the job you love. Create a schedule to support your effort so you can measure your results. Remember, what gets measured gets results!

Your schedule should include goals and accomplishments. For a job search, the important measures driving your Job Search Marketing Plan are the number of interactions you force yourself to have with people who can help you. The more interactions, the more active your job search, and the faster you get your next job.

Goals can include:

- Number of phone calls
- Number of emails to set up coffee or meetings with contacts
- Number of informational meetings
- Number of networking meetings held
- Number of LinkedIn invitations sent to new contacts
- Number of LinkedIn comments posted in Groups
- Number of Job Seeker group meetings attended
- Number of meetings in my professional group to attend.

This information goes into your daily and weekly plan. It could look like the sample schedule below.

At the beginning of the week, commit to yourself what you intend to do that week. Then keep track of what you actually accomplish. Are you doing what you said you would do? Are you keeping your commitments to yourself? If not, why not? What else are you willing to do to get what you want? Are your goals really important to you? If you are meeting your goals, can you do more? Should you challenge yourself to do more?

Review your activity charts from week to week to measure your results and see if you are putting in enough effort.

Having written goals is a great way to make progress. Doing what you say you will do can give you a great sense of accomplishment, as well as moving your job search forward.

Sample of Weekly Schedule

Goal	M	T	W	Th	F
# calls					
# emails					
# informational meetings					
# network meetings					
# LinkedIn invitations					
# LinkedIn comments					
# job seeker meetings					
#professional meetings					

Final Words to the Wise

A job search without a Job Search Marketing Plan is like wandering around without a map. You will spend time but never get anywhere. Most people cannot afford the luxury of wandering around aimlessly.

Your plan needs to be written. It can have lots of detail or only a little but it should be written with the end in mind.

Set goals for yourself each day and week then keep track of your progress. What gets measured gets results.

Know what you want and what makes you different from other candidates. This information will differentiate you from the competition for the job you want.

Know where to find the job you want. Then set out to meet the people who can help you find what you want. The more people you know and the more questions you ask, the faster you will find the job you love!

Seek out experts. By leveraging what they know, you can move your job search along faster.

Be calm, confident, and courageous and you will achieve your goal – the job you love!

Discussion Questions

There are many ways to use this book. You can create your own personal job search marketing plan if you are looking for a job right now. You can use the same steps to plan for the future. Career development is a very personal thing. Take ownership of your own career by planning for the future with your personal job search marketing plan.

We encourage you to discuss this book with others who are having a similar experience. Working together increases camaraderie and leverages the strengths of the individuals across the group. If you are not already part of a job seekers group, find one in your community and attend regularly. If you are part of a job seekers group, get more active.

Here are some questions to consider about your job search. You might find these questions interesting to discuss with your job seekers group. Use the space available to make notes and record your ideas.

1. Considering the differences between a detailed search plan and a less structured approach, which qualities of each type of search describe your current process? Focusing on the less structured aspects, what suggestions from the text can you implement to create a more detailed strategy? Create a list with several different strategies for addressing areas in your current plan that need work.

2. What are the ways you network now? Can you identify three new, different ways to network? How could you add each of these new strategies to your job search plan?

3. How has finding a job changed over the last 30 years? Share how your job search today is different from your first job search (if this is not your first job search). Review your previous job searches. Considering the information provided in the text, how would your previous searches fair in the new marketplace? What strategies would you apply now if you were looking for that same position?

4. How can LinkedIn contacts help your job search? How do you use currently use LinkedIn to meet people? Identify strategies you can utilize to make LinkedIn a more effective tool for networking. What are the advantages of having more LinkedIn contacts?

Create a list of people you know in all areas of your life – personal and professional. Pull names and email addresses from your address books. Enter all those people in LinkedIn to expand your contacts. Of those people, is there anyone who has information about the kind of job you seek?

5. How can you use the information provided in the text to help you even if you are happily employed? What steps could you take now while you have a reasonably secure position that might help you in the event of an unexpected layoff?

6. How can you increase your professional network? Make a plan that includes three or more strategies to begin or improve your networking abilities? Identify what you need to do to make these things happen?

7. Considering the example of Bill, who works for a jerk, is there some strategy that you can take away from Bill's situation that can be used to help think about the kind of workplace you want in your next position? How would you advise Bill to network so he can avoid working for a jerk? How could those strategies help you in your current position?

8. Have you ever considered doing something else? What kinds of things bring you joy? Can you find people who do those jobs? How could you use your inspirations and dreams as a way to help you find a job doing something you might really enjoy?

9. Frequently, people who cannot find a job immediately jump to the conclusion that they must be the problem? Have you ever felt this way? How does that make you feel about your prospects? What concrete steps can you take to change the internal dialog?

About The Interview Doctor, Inc. ®

Do the stories in this book sound familiar? Have you been in the same position as these people looking for a job? Are you at your wits end?

The Interview Doctor® can show you a better way.

The Interview Doctor® can save you time and effort, moving your job search ahead by miles so you can land the job you love. We have the insight because we have the personal experience finding jobs and the business experience hiring people. We know how you feel. We know what employers are looking for. We know how to break through those barriers with the right techniques to get the job you love.

We coach candidates via phone or in person - our services are available when and where you need them.

Shorten your job search. Find the job you love. Get the answers you need with personal job search coaching from The Interview Doctor®.

Become the one of the success stories. Working with The Interview Doctor® you will see results!

• Know your story and how to use it to get a job offer

- Know the important pieces to include in your resume
- Break through the Phone Screen barrier and land the job interview
- Understand how to act and what to say in the actual interview

All of these pieces play an important part in landing the job offer. When you go through our Job Interview Coaching process you will learn how to adjust your job search tactics and improve your results – resulting in Job Offers and landing the Job you love.

Contact The Interview Doctor® and get the help you need with your Job Interview and Search.

We are The Interview Doctors

Katherine Burik is an energetic and creative leader with a service focus to human resources. She has specific expertise in strategic human resource planning and coaching leadership teams to improve performance and results.

The Interview Doctor sprang from Katherine's observation, based on her human resource experience and work with recruiters that candidates need to improve their interviewing skills. She coaches candidates looking for jobs, and speaks frequently to groups about career development and successful job search techniques. Her thoughts about job search appear regularly in The Interview Doctor blog.

In her previous life as Vice President or Director of Human Resources at several businesses in Chicago and Northeast Ohio, Katherine reported to the President and CEO, responsible for the entire array of human resource functions. She has been laid off more times than most people she knows. Contrary to public opinion, being laid off can be liberating!

Katherine is a member of the Society of Human Resource Managers, the American Society of Training and Development, and the Worldwide Association of Business Coaches.

She earned her BA in History from Northwestern University and MS in Industrial Relations from Loyola University of Chicago. She has been certified as a Senior HR Professional by the Society of Human Resource Managers and is certified as a Registered Corporate Coach.

Dan Toussant is the managing director of The Interview Doctor, Inc.® As a human resource professional with over 20 years of leadership experience, specializing in management and professional recruiting, he also speaks regularly to groups about the job-seeking process, and coaches professionals of any age one-on-one regarding interviewing skills, resume preparation, and career transition. He serves as the co-editor of The Interview Doctor Blog, and teams with his business partner, Katherine Burik, and other HR professionals in this job-interviewing skills, career-coaching collaborative, The Interview Doctor.

Dan holds a master's degree in Education from Kent State University and a Bachelor's degree in English from Boston College.

He is the beneficiary of some rather unique job promotions and changes in his professional life. Staying in his hometown and still working to advance his career has led to some interesting opportunities including nine years as HR Consulting Leader with a regional CPA firm, and now as a Professional Recruiter and Job-Interviewing-Skills Webinar/Seminar Presenter and Coach.

He is an active member of Toastmasters International, Business Networking International (BNI), and the Society of Human Resource Management.

Connect with us: We want to connect with you on LinkedIn individually and at our LinkedIn Group, Job Search Check-Up.

Call the Interview Doctor® today at 800-914-7349! Sign up to receive our newsletter and blog at our website,

http://jobinterviewcoaching.org/about/.

Read on for a Preview

The Interview Doctor's next installment

The Job Seeker's Manifesto: Resumes 2.0

The Job Seeker's Manifesto: Resumes 2.0

You can tell how old someone is by their point of view regarding resumes. In the "olden days", say 15 or 20 years ago, resumes, summaries describing an individual's last few jobs and education, were typed or printed on special fancy paper purchased from the local stationary store. Laid off employees might attend an outplacement workshop to develop a final resume. At the end of the day, they received 50 copies of their new resume, printed on nice paper to begin their job search. Then off went the prospective candidate to hand out resumes and find a job.

Young people reading this are muttering to themselves, "typed?" "Fancy paper?" "Stationary store?" What the heck does that mean?

It is a sign of the times that such things have changed so much so quickly. Business has changed. The world has changed. Resumes have changed too.

You no longer need to find a secretary to type your resume professionally. You do not need special paper from a special stationary store (translation: stationary = paper) to use exclusively for business purposes.

I still have printed copies of old resumes in my file cabinet. Maybe you do too. If you do, then you probably are one of the parents who advise their children to seek out a professional to write their resume. Those parents believe that a fancy, printed resume these days is the ticket to a new job; that resumes are static and must be professionally prepared.

Don't get me wrong. Part of our service is writing resumes for people. But, the technology has changed the world. As a result, resumes have a different role in today's job search.

This book explores the new role of resumes. Resumes are one of many tools required by job searchers. However, they are not necessarily the centerpiece of today's job search as they were in the past. We will look at resumes as a part of the strategic toolbox you will assemble for your job search.

Your job search is flexible; it is personalized to your interests. Therefore, to support that job search, your tools must be flexible as well.

Chapter1: What is a Resume?

Resumes: A Description

What is a resume? What does it do?

"Resume" is a French noun meaning to continue. The job search resume is a description your employment past and your goals for your employment future.

Since a job search is a continuation of employment from one employer or job to another it makes sense that in your continuing career progression you need tools to describe what you bring to the table from your past that will make you successful in the future.

The resume provides the rationale for a transition between old and new employment Your experiences define you and support your future goals.

Resumes Then

In the old days, a resume was critical as the main way to tell people about you. Resumes used to be static, typed documents created and utilized in a manner that reflected the times. Professional secretaries typed resumes on a typewriter because that is what was available. Resumes were professionally printed on heavy bond paper that might have a nice watermark on it. We purchased extra sheets of the same paper to use for cover letters and matching mailing envelopes. We picked up the completed resumes at the stationary store or print shop in a clean brown bag where the resume stayed until you lovingly pulled one out to mail with a typed cover letter to people who might be interested in learning more about you.

If you were interested in two different areas, then you wrote up two different resumes. Changing these static resumes required retyping and reprinting. That meant that getting it right the first time was very important. This kind of resume was the main method of presenting yourself and your experience to others in a position to hire you.

Not any longer. The world is different today.

Today almost everyone has a computer, knows how to type, and can print directly on a good printer in their home office desk. That means the ability to produce a resume on the spot has changed. The ability to type and print yourself means you can produce a resume custom designed to respond to the specific position available. Each resume can highlight specific experiences that correspond to the specific position. No more static printed resumes safely stored in a brown bags waiting for the proper moment.

In the days before social media, your resume was your only way to describe yourself to potential employers. If you wanted an employer to know about your background you gave them a written resume. There was nothing else. Today a paper resume is not even necessary. You can easily get a job without a paper resume. There are so many more ways to tell your story.

"Resume" Today

A resume remains a tool, part of your strategic personal marketing plan. It is only one tool of the many tools at your disposal to share your background and experiences with potential employers.

We use the word "resume" loosely these days. A resume is not just a written document. Your "resume" is your brand. It is a sum of the information available about you that you use to draw a picture of the you that you want to show to the world. Every word should be, carefully planned for its strategic ability to highlight your strengths and make you look like the perfect candidate for the job you wan.

It is tailored to the job you are talking to employer about

A resume can be paper or virtual now. You can expand beyond the margins of two sheets of fancy bond paper.

It tells the reader what you want and why you should have it. It tells your story. It is a reflection of who you are.

A "resume" is a consistent reflection of the person you want people to see whether they encounter you in social media outlets like LinkedIn or Facebook or meet you in person at a networking event or in a formal interview with a paper resume in your hand.

The "resume" is the consistent story you tell about yourself in as many forms as are necessary to encounter the people who control the job you want.

We usually start creating your "resume" with the actual paper resume. The discipline of editing your experiences down to a one or two page format helps identify the most important information to support your goals.

⊓

Check your bookseller for

The Interview Doctor's next installment of

The Job Seeker's Manifesto: Resumes 2.0

Coming Soon!

References

[i]"Pick Yourself Up" is a popular song composed in 1936 by Jerome Kern, with lyrics by Dorothy Fields.

[ii]Berry, T. (2008). Who needs a business plan. Bplans Blog. Retrieved from http://articles.bplans.com/writing-a-business-plan/who-needs-a-business-plan/47

[iii]Fleishner, M. (1999). Ten key components of a marketing plan. Business Know How. Retrieved from http://www.businessknowhow.com/marketing/marketing-plan.htm.

[iv]Covey, S.R. (2004). The 7 habits of highly effective people: Powerful lessons in personal change. New York: Free Press.

[v] Garza, J. (2011). Are you stuck in a time warp? The Blog: Huff Post 50. November 10, 2011. Retrieved from http://www.huffingtonpost.com/jesse-garza/are-you-stuck-in-a-time-w_b_1084175.html